SALAD
CHEF

Compiled and Edited by

Judith Bosley

Cover and design by **Steve Miles**

Illustrations by **Robyn Wingert**

LEB Inc.
Boise, Idaho

Many thanks to friends and family members who sent favorite recipes and shared their views on salad making; to busy college student artists, Steve and Robyn, for their patience, and to Aaron Mockridge and Zsuzsa Csorba for finishing touches.

LEB Inc.
5375 Kendall Street
Boise, Idaho 83706

People and Salads

Picture a long, beautiful salad bar with everything on it. Now picture people walking up to the salad bar and watch what they put on their plates. Look at their finished masterpieces. There will never be two the same, either in selection or amount. Salads are as individual as their makers. I've learned a lot while compiling this book. As I asked men, women, cooks, and those who never go into the kitchen, college students and children to share their favorites with me, I learned that there is more to a salad than what is on the plate.

Families have their traditional favorite salads, and sometimes they must be served in a certain bowl. It must be on the table because "it just wouldn't be our family dinner without it." One friend told me, "We always make the same salad. I don't know that we are all that crazy about it, but we have it just the same, because we always have." Salads even have pet names. AMANDA'S SALAD in this book is known in their family as "rotten salad." When I asked why, Amanda said, "That's just what we call it."

Sometimes a salad is made for just one person attending the feast, or in honor of one no longer there to attend. How many of you have heard Mother say, "This was my grandmother's salad, or I'm making this salad because it is Tom's, Dick's or Mary's favorite?" The rest of the family gets it by default.

Some salads are just right for children who often don't care for the fancy, many-ingredient kinds because they haven't learned to like such variety yet. CINNAMON APPLESAUCE SALAD is one of these. Some salads get served often because the ingredients are usually on hand or because they can be made in a hurry like QUICK TRICK ANY FLAVOR and ICE CREAM SALAD.

Let's have lunch together at the salad bar. I will start with a little lettuce, add a lot of spinach, shredded carrots, sprouts, green pepper, onion, mushrooms, a dollop of cottage cheese, a little dribble of ranch-style dressing, and some seeds on top. What will you have?

SALADS
Fruit

Vegetable, vegetable with meat, vegetable with fish

Pasta, pasta and meat, pasta and fish

Relishes

Salad Dressings

Fruit
Salads

1 STRAWBERRY PRETZEL SALAD

A delicious crunchy crust for this dessert salad

1 C crushed pretzels
1 1/2 T sugar
4 T margarine
1, 3 oz pkg cream cheese
1/2 C sugar

1, 8 oz frozen whipped topping
1, 3 oz pkg strawberry gelatin
1 C boiling water
1, 10 oz box frozen strawberries

Mix pretzels with 1 1/2 T sugar and soft margarine. Press mixture into a greased 8X8 inch pan. Bake at 350° for 10 minutes. Cool. Combine sugar and softened cream cheese, and fold in thawed topping. Spread over crust. Dissolve gelatin in water and add frozen berries stirring to break up berries. Pour berries over topping and chill until set. Recipe may be doubled.

2 ELEGANT PEAR MOLD

1, 16 oz can syrup-packed
   pear halves
1, 3 oz pkg lime
   gelatin

1, 3 oz pkg cream cheese
2 C whipped topping or
   whipped cream
fresh fruit for garnish

Drain pears, reserving syrup. Add water to syrup to make 1 cup.
Heat syrup mixture to boiling; remove from heat, add gelatin and
stir until dissolved. Cool slightly. Combine gelatin mixture and
cream cheese in blender and process until smooth. Add drained
pears and process only until pears are coarsely chopped.
Refrigerate pear mixture until just slightly set. Gently fold in
whipped topping. Spoon into 6-cup mold and refrigerate until
firm, 3-4 hours. Unmold onto cold plate; garnish with fresh fruit
such as melon balls, black cherries, peaches or pear slices.
Serves 4-6.

3 BLUEBERRY SALAD SQUARES

Picture pretty

2, 3 oz pkgs blackberry gelatin
1/2 C sugar
1, 15 oz can blueberries
1, 8 oz can crushed pineapple

1, 8 oz pkg cream cheese
1 C sour cream
1/2 C chopped nuts

Dissolve gelatin in 2 cups boiling water. Measure juices from berries and pineapple; add water to make 1 cup liquid and add to gelatin. Stir in fruit and chill in a flat dish until firm. Beat sour cream, cream cheese and sugar until fluffy; spread over congealed fruit. Sprinkle nuts on top. Cut in squares to serve. Serves 8.

4 LEMON SOUR CREAM MOLD

Shows the beauty of the fruit

1, 3 oz pkg lemon
   gelatin
1 C boiling water
1/2 C half-and-half or
   light cream
1/2 t vanilla

1/2 C sour cream
fresh fruit (grapes, melon balls,
   strawberries, blackberries, etc.)
mint sprigs

Dissolve gelatin in boiling water in large bowl. Stir in half-and-half and vanilla; blend in sour cream. (Mixture will appear slightly curdled.) Refrigerate until slightly thickened. Beat until mixture is smooth. Pour into 3-cup mold. Refrigerate until firm, about 3 hours. Unmold onto cold plate; surround with fresh fruit and mint sprigs.

5 EUNICE'S SALAD

You choose the fruits

1, 6 oz pkg vanilla pudding mix, not instant
1, 3 oz pkg vanilla tapioca pudding mix
3 C fuit juice, flavor of choice

4 C fruit: Diced peaches, sliced bananas, halved grapes, sliced strawberries, blueberries, pineapple tidbits, or kiwi

Combine both pudding mixes with fruit juice and cook until mixture bubbles. Cool and add fruits of choice. Salad keeps well. Serves 8.

6 STRAWBERRY BANANA SALAD

Two all time favorites combined

2, 3 oz pkg strawberry gelatin
2 C boiling water
2, 10 oz pkgs frozen strawberries
1, 1 lb can crushed pineapple with juice
3-4 mashed bananas
1 C sour cream
1/2 C nutmeats

Add water to gelatin and stir to dissolve. Stir in frozen berries,
pineapple and bananas. Pour half of mixture into an oiled mold or
9X13 pan; chill until set. Spread mixture with sour cream and
sprinkle with nuts. Add remaining fruit and chill until set.
Serves 12.

7 AMANDA'S SALAD

A family favorite

1, 3 oz pkg lime gelatin
1 C boiling water
1, 9 oz can crushed pineapple
   drained and juice reserved

1 C cottage cheese
1/2 C mayonnaise
1/4 C chopped nuts
lettuce leaves
fresh fruit

Dissolve gelatin in boiling water; add pineapple juice. Pour into a 6-cup mold or glass dish. Chill until slightly thickened. Beat until frothy. Fold in remaining ingredients. Chill until firm. Unmold onto cold plate lined with lettuce. Garnish with fresh fruit.

8 FIVE CUP SALAD

Just multiply to make any amount

1 C drained mandarin oranges
1 C drained crushed pineapple
1 C flaked coconut
1 C minature marshmallows
1 C dairy sour cream

Combine ingredients until blended. Chill and garnish as desired.
8-10 servings.

9 CHERRY COLA SALAD

Use diet cola to save calories

1, 1 lb can dark sweet cherries
1 C crushed pineapple
2, 3 oz pkgs cherry gelatin
1, 12 oz can cherry cola beverage
1 C chopped nuts, if desired

Drain fruits reserving juices; add enough water to juice to make two cups. Heat to boiling. Dissolve gelatin in boiling juice, then add cola. Chill until partially set; stir in fruits and nuts. Chill until firm.

10 WINTER FRUIT SALAD

Sweet and creamy

2 C canned peach slices
2 C canned pineapple chunks
1 C green seedless grapes
2 bananas, sliced

1 C pitted dates
1 C peach yogurt
1/4 C orange juice
1/2 t curry powder

Drain pineapple chunks and slice bananas into the pineapple juice to keep them from turning brown. Drain juice from bananas. Combine all fruits. Stir orange juice into yogurt and add curry powder to taste. Mix yogurt lightly into fruit. Serve on lettuce leaves. Serves 6.

11 PEACH PIE SALAD

Make this all year round

2, 11 oz cans mandarin oranges, drained
1, 16 oz can pineapple tidbits, drained
1, 10 oz pkg frozen sliced strawberries, with juice
1 , 20 oz can peach pie filling
3-4 sliced bananas

Mix together thoroughly; place in a clear glass bowl and chill.
Serves 6-8.

12 RAINBOW FRUIT SALAD BOWL

Have it your own way

1 pint fresh strawberries
2 pints fresh blueberries
1 medium cantaloupe*
1 honeydew melon
1/2 C orange juice**
1/2 C lemon juice

2 T sugar
1 T chopped mint leaves or
1 t dried mint, crumbled
2 kiwi fruits, sliced
1 C green or red grapes
mint sprigs,

Slice 2 large strawberries and reserve. Combine strawberries and 1/2 of the blueberries in a glass serving dish. Layer melon balls on top of strawberry mixture. Top with remaining blueberries. Blend orange juice, lemon juice, sugar and chopped mint; pour over fruit. Arrange kiwi and sliced strawberries on top. Refrigerate 2-3 hours. Garnish with grapes and mint sprigs. Serves 12.

*1 lb frozen melon balls, thawed and drained, can be substituted for the 2 melons; other fruits in season, canned or frozen fruits may be used.
**Gingerale may be substituted for juice mixture.

13 CREAMY LAYERED FRUIT SALAD

Combine these or other fruits to serve a crowd

2 C sliced peaches
2 C blueberries
2 C sliced strawberries
2 C green seedless grapes
2 C pineapple tidbits
2 small bananas, sliced

Topping:
1, 8 oz carton strawberry yogurt
1, 3 oz pkg cream cheese
1 T sugar
1 t lemon juice
2 C frozen whipped topping
1/2 t almond extract

Thaw frozen topping and combine with yogurt, softened cream cheese, sugar, lemon juice and extract; beat until smooth. Refrigerate. In a clear glass bowl, layer half of each fruit; spoon half of the topping over fruits. Layer remaining fruits and cover with rest of topping. Garnish with mint leaves. Refrigerate until serving time. Serves 20.

14 GLORIFIED RICE

For Christmas, use red and green cherries

16 ozs frozen whipped topping, or 1 pt whipping cream
1-1 1/2 C crushed pineapple, drained
2 C cold cooked rice
1 C miniature marshmallows
1/2 C maraschino cherries, quartered
sugar or sweetener to taste

Thaw topping or whip cream and fold in rest of ingredients. Add sugar to taste. Pile lightly in serving dish, and decorate with cherries. Chill. Serves 12.

15 STRAWBERRY POPPYSEED SALAD

The secret of this delicious salad is the dressing

lettuce: any combination of Bibb, Romaine, and head lettuce
sliced fresh strawberries
toasted almonds, pecans or walnuts

Arrange lettuce, berries and nuts on individual salad plates. Top with poppyseed dressing.

Poppyseed Dressing:
1 C mayonnaise
4 T vinegar
1/2-2/3 C sugar

1/2 C milk
2 t poppyseed

Shake dressing ingredients in a jar and serve.

16 CINNAMON APPLESAUCE SALAD

Loved by children of every age

1, 6 oz pkg red gelatin
2 C boiling water

1/4 C cinnamon candies
1, #2 can applesauce

Dissolve candies in boiling water and add gelatin. Stir in applesauce. *This salad varies in consistency depending on thickness of applesauce. If applesauce is very thick, add 1/4 C cold water to gelatin.* Pour into a clear glass bowl or oiled ring mold. Center of ring mold is pretty filled with cottage cheese.

17 QUICK TRICK ANY FLAVOR SALAD

1 lb cottage cheese
1, 3 oz pkg gelatin, any flavor

1, #2 can crushed pineapple
1, 12 oz carton whipped
topping

Stir dry gelatin into cottage cheese; stir in undrained pineapple and thawed topping. Pour mixture into serving bowl and garnish as desired. Serves 8.

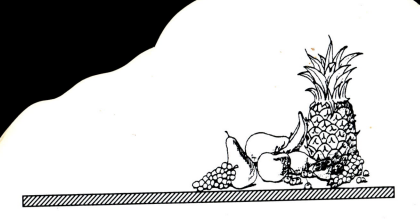

18 CHRISTMAS SALAD

Pretty enough for a red and white centerpiece

1, 3 oz pkg lemon gelatin
1, 3 oz pkg cherry gelatin
1, 21 oz can cherry pie filling
1, 3 oz pkg cream cheese
1/3 C mayonnaise

1 C crushed pineapple
 (with juice)
1 C whipped topping
1 C miniature marshmallows
1 T chopped nuts

Dissolve cherry gelatin in one cup boiling water; add pie filling and pour mixture in an oiled mold. Chill. Dissolve lemon gelatin in one cup boiling water. Mix softened cream cheese and mayonnaise and add to hot gelatin. Stir in pineapple, whipped topping, marshmallows and nuts. Pour mixture over cherries in mold and chill until set. Unmold on a clear glass plate. Serves 12.

19 BANANA PEANUT SALAD

3 lg sliced bananas
Dressing:
2 T butter
3 beaten eggs
1/2 C sugar

3 T chopped peanuts

2 T flour
1 C pineapple or orange juice

Combine dressing ingredients and cook over low heat until thickened and smooth. Chill until completely cold. On salad plates layer sliced bananas, spoon on dressing and top with nuts. Serves 4-5.

20 ICE CREAM SALAD

You decide the flavor and color

1, 3 oz pkg gelatin
1 C boiling water

1, 10 oz pkg frozen fruit
1 C vanilla ice cream

Dissolve gelatin in water; stir in berries and ice cream. Refrigerate for 20 minutes. Serves 4.

21 HAM 'N FRUIT SALAD

A main dish salad

1 1/2 C diced ham
1, 1 lb can pineapple tidbits
1 C sliced celery
1/2 C dry roasted peanuts
1/2 C raisins
1/2 t salt

Dressing:
pineapple juice
1 T lemon juice
1 egg, beaten
1/3 C sugar
1 T cornstarch

Drain pineapple, reserving juice. Mix ham, pineapple, raisins, celery and nuts. Heat pineapple and lemon juice in a saucepan. Blend sugar and cornstarch and stir into hot juice to thicken. Whip beaten egg into hot dressing. Cool to lukewarm and fold into fruit and ham mixture. Chill. Serves 8.

22 CRANBERRY MARSHMALLOW SALAD

2 C raw cranberries
4 C miniature marshmallows
1/2 C sugar

1/4 C chopped apple
1/2 C chopped nuts
1 C whipping cream,

Grind cranberries or process with a food processor; stir in marshmallows and sugar and let chill overnight. Whip cream and fold into mixture with nuts and apple. Pile each serving on a pineapple slice. Serves 12.

23 APPLESAUCE RASPBERRY SALAD

1, 3 oz pkg raspberry gelatin
1, 10 oz pkg frozen raspberries
1 C unsweetened applesauce

1 C sour cream
1 C tiny marshmallows

Dissolve gelatin in 1 C boiling water. Add frozen raspberries and stir until thawed. Stir in applesauce. Pour into 10x6 inch baking dish and chill until set. Combine sour cream and marshmallows and spread on top of gelatin. Cover and chill 1-2 hours more. Cut into squares and serve on lettuce leaves. Serves 6.

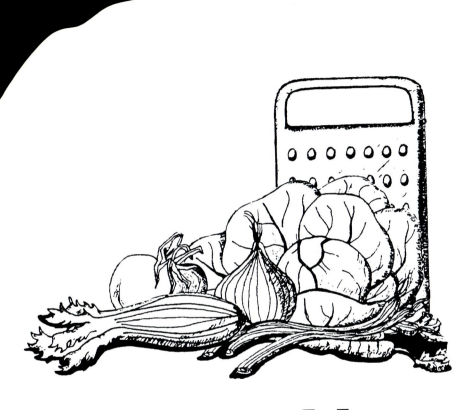

Vegetable
Salads

24 CORN AND RICE SALAD

Great color and flavor

2 C canned whole kernel corn
2 C cooked rice
1/4 C chopped sweet pepper
1/4 C sliced green onion
1/4 C ripe olives
3 T vinegar

2 T soy sauce
1 T dried parsley
1/2 t Dijon mustard
1/4 t garlic powder
1 1/2 C diced tomatoes
1 T Parmesan cheese

Combine ingredients and mix well. Cover and chill for several hours. Serves 8.

25 MARINATED RICE SALAD

Marinate overnight for unique flavor

1 C cooked brown or white rice
1/2 C bottled Italian dressing
1 T soy sauce
1/2 t sugar
2 C shredded spinach
1/2 C sliced green onions, with tops
1/2 C chopped celery
1/2 C crumbled crisp bacon

Mix dressing with rice; add soy sauce and sugar. Cover and refrigerate over night. Just before serving add remaining ingredients. Serves 4.

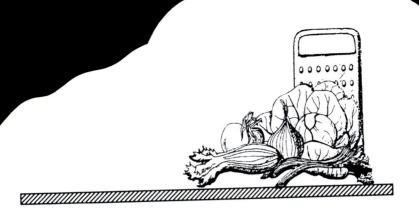

26 SWEET & SOUR BROCCOLI SALAD

8 C raw broccoli flowerettes
1 C raisins
1 C sliced mushrooms
1/2 C chopped red onion
6 slices crisp bacon, crumbled
salt and pepper
Dressing:
1 large egg
1 egg yolk

1/2 C sugar
1/2 t dry mustard
1 1/2 t cornstarch
1/2 C white vinegar
1/4 C water
1/4 t salt
2 T butter
1/2 C mayonnaise

Combine salad ingredients. For dressing, whisk together egg, yolk, sugar, mustard and cornstarch; add mixture to vinegar, water and salt in sauce pan and cook for 1 minute. Stir in butter and mayonnaise. Pour warm mixture over salad. Cover and chill. Serves 8-10.

27 CRUNCHY CABBAGE SALAD

Different and delicious

1 medium head cabbage, shredded
4 sliced green onions
1 pkg Ramen soup mix

1 T sugar
salt to taste
1/2 t pepper

Dressing:
3 T red wine vinegar
1/2 C salad oil

1/2 C sliced almonds
2 T sesame seeds

Shred cabbage very finely and add sliced onions. Toast almonds and sesame seeds in 350°oven until lightly browned. Mix dressing ingredients and add seasonings from packet in soup mix; pour over cabbage and toss well. Add seeds and almonds. Crumble crisp noodles from soup packet over salad just before serving and toss again. Serves 8.

28 PLAIN GOOD COLD SLAW

A cabbage lovers favorite

5 C shredded cabbage
3/4 C shredded carrots
1/2 C chopped green pepper
1/4 C minced onion

1/2-1C salad dressing
1-2 t vinegar
1-2 t sugar
salt and pepper to taste

Combine cabbage, green peppers, carrots and onions in large bowl. Combine salad dressing, vinegar, sugar, salt and pepper in small bowl, stir to blend. Add dressing to cabbage mixture and toss lightly. Let stand and toss again. Serves 6-8.

29 CABBAGE CARROT SLAW

4 C shredded cabbage
4 C shredded carrot
1 C raisins
1 C mayonnaise

4 T honey
1 t grated lemon rind
4 T lemon juice
1/2 t ground ginger

Mix dressing ingredients and toss with cabbage, carrots and raisins. Chill. Serves 12.

30 CABBAGE CRUNCH SALAD

Spanish peanuts add a nice touch

1, 15 oz can kidney beans
2 C shredded cabbage
1 C sliced celery
1 C sliced radishes
1 C sliced water chestnuts
1 C sliced cucumber
1 1/2-2 C salad dressing

1 C frozen peas
1/4 C minced onion
1/2 C diced green pepper
1 C sliced green olives
salt and pepper
1 C Spanish peanuts

Drain beans and water chestnuts, thaw and drain peas. Mix all ingredients except peanuts and chill. At serving time add peanuts, reserving a few for garnish. Toss well and place in a large serving bowl lined with lettuce leaves. Sprinkle with reserved peanuts. Serves 12-15.

31 RED SWEET AND SOUR COLD SLAW

1 head red cabbage, shredded
6 slices bacon
3 T bacon drippings
2 T chopped onion

1 t cornstarch
1 t salt
1/2 C packed brown sugar
1/3 C white vinegar
1/4 C water

Fry bacon until crisp; drain and crumble. Cook onion in bacon fat and add remaining ingredients except bacon and cabbage. Cook, stirring constantly until clear. Cool, add bacon and pour over cabbage, mixing well. Let stand overnight. Serves 12.

32 KIDNEY BEAN SALAD

1, 1 lb can kidney beans, drained
2 hard boiled eggs, chopped
1/3 C chopped sweet pickle
salt and pepper

1/4 C sliced celery
3 T minced onion
1/4-1/3 C mayonnaise
1 C warm cooked rice
(optional)

Mix ingredients and chill before serving. Serves 6.

33 TWO BEAN SALAD

1, #2 can small lima beans
1, #2 can yellow wax beans
1/2 C sliced black olives
1/4 C chopped pimiento

1/4 C chopped onion
2/3 C vinegar
1/3 C oil
1/2-3/4 C brown sugar

Combine drained beans with olives, pimiento and onions. Mix remaining ingredients and pour over bean mixture. Refrigerate for several hours to blend flavors.

34 THREE BEAN SALAD

Easy and low calorie; needs no dressing

1, 16 oz can pork and beans
1, 8 oz can cut green beans
1, 8 oz can yellow beans

2 T vinegar
1/3 C minced onion
salt and pepper

Drain liquid from all beans, combine ingredients and chill. 4 Cups.

*See **Relishes** for marinated vegetable and bean salads

35 MEXICAN SALAD BOWL

Quick to put together for lunch

1/2 C mayonnaise
1/4 C minced green onion
2 T chili sauce
2 t vinegar
1 t onion salt

1/2 t chili powder
4 drops hot pepper sauce
1, 16 oz can whole kernel corn
1, 15 oz can kidney beans
1/2 C sliced black olives

Drain beans and corn well. Mix first seven ingredients; add corn, beans and olives to dressing and stir to blend. Chill. Serves 6.

36 JEAN'S ASPARAGUS SALAD MOLD

Unusual and delicious

1 can asparagus soup
1, 8 oz pkg cream cheese
3/4 C chopped celery
1/2 C chopped nuts
1/2 C mayonnaise

1, 3 oz pkg lime gelatin
1 t grated onion
1/2 C chopped green pepper
1/4 C cold water
6 stalks fresh asparagus

Slice asparagus thinly and cook just until tender-crisp; drain and cool. Heat soup and stir in gelatin, cheese and mayonnaise until smooth. Add remaining ingredients, and pour mixture into prepared mold. Chill. Serves 8-10

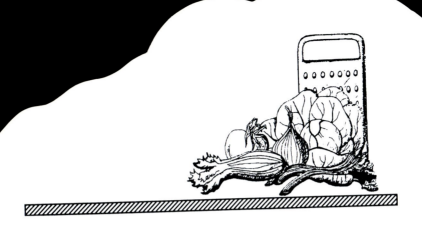

37 MOLDED CUCUMBER SALAD

A tangy salad to serve with ham

1 lb cottage cheese
1 small onion, finely diced
1/2 C salad dressing
1 t vinegar
1 medium unpeeled cucumber, very finely diced
1, 3 oz pkg lemon gelatin

Prepare vegetables and mix with cheese, salad dressing and
vinegar. Dissolve gelatin in water and immediately stir in cheese
mixture. Pour into flat serving dish or greased mold and chill until
set. Serves 6.

38 CARROT AND RAISIN SALAD

Pretty and crunchy

2 C shredded carrot
1/3-1/2 C dark raisins
1/4 C Spanish peanuts

1/2 t salt
1/2 C mayonnaise

Mix altogether. Add mayonnaise to desired consistency. Chill.

39 PEAS AND PEANUTS

A delicious concoction to serve with pork

1 C salted Spanish peanuts
1/4 C mayonnaise
1/4 C sour cream

1 C frozen peas
1 T lemon juice
1/2 t minced onion

Thaw and drain peas. Mix with remaining ingredients and chill.

40 SLIVERED EGG SALAD

A tasty, low calorie dish to serve warm

4 eggs
1 t soy sauce
1 t sugar
1 t salt

1 T oil
1/2 C sliced mushrooms
1 C sliced celery
4 C shredded lettuce
1/2 C sliced green onion

Beat eggs with soy sauce, sugar and salt. Pour in four portions into a large sprayed skillet, and cook quickly, turning once. Cool on a plate, then roll the four pancakes together and slice into thin strips. Heat oil in a fry pan or wok. Stir fry mushrooms with celery and onions briefly. Add lettuce and egg strips and stir just until heated. Season with additional soy sauce, sugar and salt to taste. Serves 4.

41 PLAIN GOOD POTATO SALAD

The secret is lots of eggs and mixing while warm

6 C warm, cooked potatoes*
6 hard cooked eggs (may be cooked with the potatoes)
1/3 C diced onion, or more to taste
1 1/2 C salad dressing
1/2 C milk
1 T vinegar or pickle juice
2 t sugar
salt and pepper to taste

Chop potatoes and eggs together; stir in onion. Combine salad dressing with milk; stir in vinegar and sugar and pour over potatoes. (Mixture should be quite moist and will thicken as it chills.) Garnish with sliced eggs, green pepper slices, black olive slices, paprika or other garnish as desired for color.

*Cooked cauliflower may be substitued for potato.

42 DILLED POTATO SALAD

Pretty red salad, leave the skins on

4 lbs small red potatoes
1 T vinegar
1 T oil
1 C minced red onion
salt and pepper to taste

1 C plain yogurt
1/2-1 C mayonnaise
1 T Dijon mustard
2 T dill weed

Cook and drain potatoes. Cut in quarters, sprinkle with oil and vinegar and toss lightly to coat. Chill to blend flavors. Combine mayonnaise, yogurt and mustard, and thin slightly with a little milk. Add mustard and seasonings and pour over potatoes, tossing gently to mix. Cover and chill. Serves 10.

43 CORNED BEEF HASH SALAD

A main dish salad to serve with Irish soda bread

3 C finely diced, cooked potatoes
1, 12 oz can corned beef
2 T chopped sweet pickles
2 C slightly cooked frozen peas
2 T pickle juice
2 T prepared horseradish
1 C mayonnaise or salad dressing

Dice corned beef and combine with pickle, potatoes and peas. Mix pickle juice with horseradish and mayonnaise. Mix dressing with other ingredients.

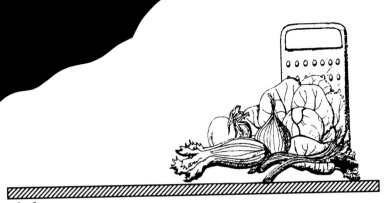

44 GERMAN POTATO SALAD

Our family's favorite

6 medium potatoes
6 slices bacon
1/3 C bacon fat
3/4 C sliced onion
2 T flour
1-2 T sugar
1 1/2 t salt
1/4 t pepper
3/4 C water
1/3 C vinegar

Boil potatoes in skins; cool, peel and slice. Fry bacon until crisp, drain on paper towel and reserve fat. Cook onion in 1/3 cup bacon fat until yellow; mix in flour and sugar, then add remaining ingredients. Cook, stirring until mixture boils. Boil one minute. Pour over potatoes and add crumbled bacon, reserving some for garnish. Keep salad warm in a crock pot or over hot water. Serve warm. Serves 8.

45 BACON LETTUCE AND TOMATO SALAD

A country club favorite

romaine lettuce leaves
1/2 head lettuce
3 ripe tomatoes
1 C croutons

8 slices bacon
1/2 C mayonnaise
salt and pepper

Cook bacon until crisp; drain and crumble. Line salad bowl with romaine. Break head lettuce into bite-sized pieces. Cut tomatoes into wedges and add with bacon to head lettuce. Add mayonnaise and toss lightly; season to taste with salt and pepper and pile in salad bowl. Serves 4-6.

To make your own croutons, toast bread cubes in slow oven, 225° until dry.

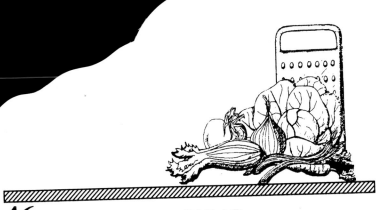

46 SEVEN LAYER SALAD

Count this any way you like

1 head lettuce, cut up
1 C thinly sliced celery
1 small onion, chopped
1 green pepper, chopped
1, 10 oz pkg frozen peas
2 C salad dressing
2 T sugar
1/2 lb bacon, fried, drained and crumbled
1 C shredded cheddar cheese*

Assemble salad in order given in container that may be used for serving. Peas may be added frozen. Use no salt. Apply salad dressing with a spatula. Chill for 12 hours before serving. Serves 12.

Additional or alternate layers: Chopped boiled egg, diced tomato, black olives, water chestnuts and shredded carrot.

47 TOM & CINDY'S SUPER SALAD

Hide it until dinner

1 head cauliflower
1 head broccoli
1/4 lb bacon
1 medium red onion

1/3 C Parmesan cheese
1/3 C sugar
1 C mayonnaise

Break or cut cauliflower and broccoli into bite-sized pieces. Separate red onion slices into rings and add to vegetables. Fry bacon until crisp, drain and crumble. Add crumbled bacon, cheese and sugar to vegetables. Toss mixture with mayonnaise and chill for several hours before serving. Toss again and place in serving bowl. Serves 8-10.

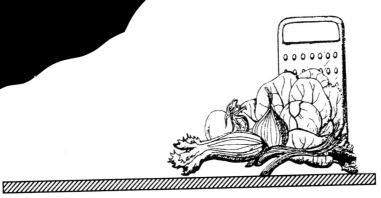

48 WILTED SPINACH SALAD

The classic spinach salad

1, 10 oz pkg fresh spinach*
4 green onions
coarsely ground black pepper
6-8 slices bacon, diced
1/4 C wine vinegar

2 T sugar
1/2 t salt
1/2 lb sliced mushrooms
4 hard-boiled eggs

Wash spinach, discard stems and pat dry; tear into bite-sized pieces and place in salad bowl. Slice onions with tops and slice mushrooms; add to spinach. Grind pepper over vegetables. Just before serving, fry bacon bits; add vinegar, sugar and salt. Pour hot mixture over spinach and toss until coated and slightly wilted. Sprinkle with chopped eggs. Serves 4-6.

*To make WILTED LETTUCE SALAD, eliminate mushrooms, substitute 1 head lettuce or 8 C leaf lettuce for spinach and use 2 tablespoons brown sugar in dressing. Season to taste. Use just two eggs as garnish.

49 SPINACH BEAN SPROUT SALAD

2, 10 oz pkgs spinach
1, 16 oz can bean sprouts
5 hard boiled eggs
1 lb bacon
1 C sliced black olives
3/4 lb fresh mushrooms, sliced
6 sliced green onions
1/2 C sliced water chestnuts

Dressing:
1/2 C oil
2/3 C sugar
1/3 C catsup
1/4 t salt
1/4 C red wine vinegar
1 T Worcestershire sauce
1 medium onion, chopped

Puree dressing ingredients in blender. Trim spinach stems, wash and dry between towels and refrigerate to crisp. Fry bacon, drain and crumble. Drain bean sprouts, and chop eggs. At serving time, combine salad ingredients and toss with dressing. Serves 8-10.

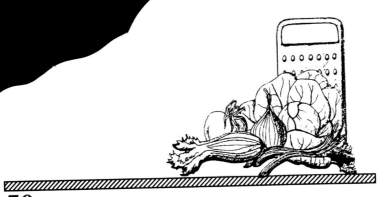

50 APPLE & MEAT SALAD

A good use for leftover roast

2 C cooked meat, diced
1 C sliced celery
1 C diced unpeeled apple

1/4 C mayonnaise
1 T prepared mustard
1/2 t salt

Combine mayonnaise, mustard and salt; add meat, celery and apple to dressing and stir to blend. Adjust seasoning. Serve on lettuce leaves. Serves 5.

51 MOLDED CORNED BEEF SALAD

1 C corned beef
1 green pepper, diced
1 C sliced celery
1 small onion, diced
1/2 t salt

1 T lemon juice
1 C salad dressing
1 t sugar
1/2 C chopped nuts
1, 3 oz pkg lemon gelatin

Dissolve gelatin in 1 cup boiling water, add 3/4 C cold water and chill until slightly set; add all other ingredients, place in a mold and chill until set. Serves 8.

52 COLD CHILI SALAD

A good use for cold roast beef

1/3 C salad dressing
1/4 C catsup
2 T minced green pepper
2 C cubed cooked beef
salt, pepper and chili powder to taste

1 C sliced celery
1/2 C chopped onion
2 hard cooked eggs, chopped

Blend all ingredients and chill to blend flavors. Serves 5.

53 PEPPER STEAK SALAD

3 C rare roast beef strips
2 C cooked rice
1 large green pepper cut in rings
1 C sliced celery
5 greens onions with tops, sliced
1 C fresh or canned bean sprouts

5 sliced fresh mushrooms
1/2 C teriyaki sauce
1/3 C salad oil
1/3 C dry sherry
3 T red wine vinegar

Combine teriyaki sauce, oil, sherry, and vinegar; pour over rest of ingredients. Chill to blend flavors. Serves 10.

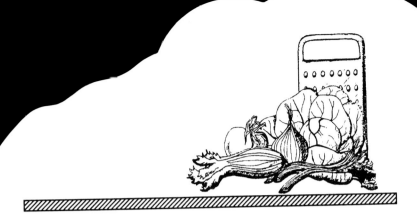

54 LEMONY BEEF SALAD

A deluxe dinner salad for 4

2 C roast beef strips
1 C sliced fresh mushrooms
2 tomatoes, cut in wedges
1 head lettuce, or leaf lettuce
2/3 C sour cream
1 t Dijon mustard

1/4 C lemon juice
2 T water
2 T sugar
1 t poppy seed
1/2 t salt

Bring lemon juice, water, sugar, poppy seed and salt to a boil, and simmer for a few minutes. Pour hot mixture over beef and mushrooms and let stand for 2-3 hours. Drain marinade from beef and reserve 3 tablespoons. Blend mustard, sour cream and reserved marinade. To assemble salads: Arrange torn lettuce on salad plates; top with meat mixture. Garnish with tomatoes. Serve sour cream dressing on the side. 4 Servings.

55 TACO SALAD

One of the many varieties of this favorite

1 head lettuce, shredded
1/2 C chopped onion
1/2 C chopped green pepper
2 medium tomatoes, chopped
1 lb ground beef
1, #2 can red beans

1 C shredded yellow cheese
1 C buttermilk
1 C mayonnaise
1 pkg taco seasoning mix
corn chips, plain or taco
flour tortilla cups (optional)

Brown ground beef and drain well; drain and rinse beans and add to beef. Layer lettuce, onion, pepper and tomato in salad bowl. Spoon meat mixture over all and sprinkle with cheese. Combine buttermilk, mayonnaise and taco seasoning mix; pour over salad and toss. Crush corn chips and toss with salad. *Dressing and corn chips may be served on the side. Salad may be served in tortilla cups. To make tortilla cups: Soften tortillas in microwave for a few seconds and press into sprayed oven proof sauce dishes six inches in diameter. Place dishes on a baking sheet and bake shells in a 350° oven, 10-12 minutes or until crisp. Let cool.* Serves 12.

56   CHEF SALAD SUPREME

A crowd pleaser!

2 heads lettuce
2 heads endive
2 C cottage cheese
2 C cubed cooked ham
2 C cubed cooked turkey
1 C crumbed blue cheese
8 hard boiled eggs, sliced

1/2 C sliced green onions
1 C shredded carrot
1/2 C raisins
1 C sliced mushrooms
1 C shredded cheddar
1 C shredded Provolone
  cheese

Tear half of lettuce into large salad bowls. Layer half of all ingredients, rest of lettuce and rest of toppings. Serve with several bottled dressings. Serves 12 or more.

57 LAYERED TURKEY SALAD

1 medium head lettuce
1, 20 oz can white kidney beans
1 small red onion
3 C cooked turkey
2 small zucchini, sliced

1 C shredded Jack cheese,
1/2 lb salami
2 C cherry tomatoes, halved
2 C mayonnaise
2 T prepared mustard
1 t prepared horseradish

Tear lettuce in bite-sized pieces; drain beans, slice onion and separate into rings, slice salami thinly and quarter slices, and halve tomatoes. Place about 1/2 of the lettuce in large glass bowl. Top with a layer of beans, onion, turkey, sliced zucchini, cheese, salami remaining lettuce and tomatoes. Mix mayonnaise, mustard and horseradish; spread over tomatoes, sealing to edge of bowl. Cover and refrigerate at least 8 hours. Serves 10.

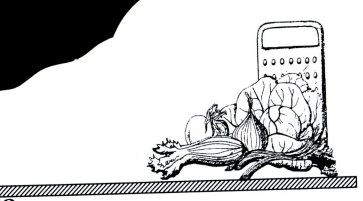

58 HOT TURKEY SALAD

2 C cooked turkey,
  cut-up
2 C plain croutons
2 C sliced celery
1 C mayonnaise

1/2 C slivered almonds
2 T lemon juice
1 T onion, chopped fine
1/2 t salt
1/2 C shredded cheese

Mix all ingredients except 1 cup of croutons and cheese. Pour into greased 2-quart casserole. Sprinkle with remaining croutons and cheese. Bake at 350° for 30-35 minutes. Serves 6.

59 HOT CHICKEN SALAD

2 C cooked chicken
1, #2 can chop suey vegetables
1 C sliced water chestnuts
1 can cream of chicken soup
1/2 C mayonnaise

1 T chopped onion
1 T lemon juice
1 T dried parsley
salt and pepper to taste
1 C crushed potato chips

Combine ingredients in a greased casserole dish, using potato chips as topping. Serves 6-8.

60 FAVORITE CHICKEN SALAD

*Keep everything on hand and have a
gourmet lunch for guests in just minutes.*

1 head lettuce, chopped
2 C diced cooked chicken*
1/2 C sliced almonds
3 T sesame seeds
canned chow mein noodles

Dressing:
8 T sugar
8 T vinegar
2 t salt
1/2 t black pepper
3/4 t MSG
1/2 C oil

Toast almonds and sesame seed in a dry skillet until golden. Cool.
Combine dressing ingredients except oil and bring to a boil; cool
and add to oil. To assemble salad, place 1/2 C chicken on a thick
bed of lettuce on each plate; sprinkle with nuts, seeds, and noodles.
Shake dressing well and pour sparingly over salad. Serve with
garlic toast. Serves 4.

* Also good with tuna and salmon

61 CHICKEN & CUCUMBER SALAD

A pretty, low calorie lunch for 4

1 frying chicken, skinned, cooked, boned, cut into chunks
2 cucumbers, peeled, cubed
1 red sweet pepper, chopped

1 T vinegar
1/2 t salt
1/4 t pepper
1/4 t seasoned salt
4 oz plain non-fat yogurt

In medium bowl, mix cucumber and sweet pepper; sprinkle with vinegar, salt and pepper. Let stand for 5 minutes. Stir in chicken, seasoned salt and yogurt, tossing gently. Cover and refrigerate until completely chilled. Serve on dark curly endive. Serves 4.

62 CHICKEN SALAD WITH CAPERS

Different, delicious and beautiful

3 chicken breast quarters
1/4 C olive oil
1 1/2 t oregano
juice of 1 lemon
3/4 C sliced black olives

2 T capers
8-10 cherry tomatoes
1/4 lb fresh green beans
salt and pepper

Cover chicken with water and add: One chopped onion, 1 teaspoon thyme, 1 bayleaf, 1 tablespoon dried parsley, a few whole cloves and peppercorns. Cook until chicken is done and let meat cool in broth in refrigerator.

Shred cold chicken, discarding broth. Steam green beans until tender crisp. Halve tomatoes. Combine chicken with remaining ingredients and chill. Serves 8.

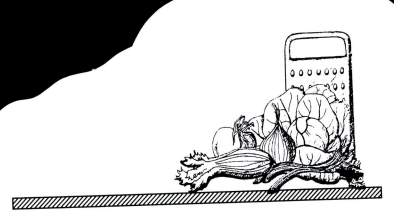

63 CHICKEN STUFFED TOMATOES

Picture pretty salads for two, four or more

2 C cooked chicken, cut in thin strips
2 hard boiled eggs
1 T chopped onion
1 C diced celery
1/4 C mayonnaise
salt and pepper to taste
4 medium-sized ripe tomatoes
shredded lettuce
dried or fresh parsley

Combine chicken, eggs, onion, celery and mayonnaise. Season to taste. Wash and core tomatoes. Slash each tomato into six wedges, not cutting all the way to the bottom. Pull wedges apart and place each tomato on a pile of shredded lettuce on a salad plate. Pile chicken salad mixture lightly on tomato. Garnish with parsley. Cut recipe in half to serve 2. Double recipe to serve 8.

64 CURRIED CHICKEN SALAD

Fruit and spice with chicken is nice

2 medium tart apples
1 T lemon juice
2 C diced chicken
2 C diced celery
1 C chopped pecans
2 t minced onion

1 C mayonnaise
1 t salt
1/2 t paprika
2 t curry powder
4 hard boiled eggs

Peel and chop apples; cover apples with water and add one teaspoon lemon juice. Drain apples and combine with chicken, celery and pecans. Chop eggs and add to chicken mixture with remaining ingredients; toss lightly. Serves 8-10.

65 CHICKEN WALDORF DIET SALAD

Low calorie and tasty

1/4 C lowfat yogurt
1 T sour cream
1/2 t grated orange rind
salt and pepper to taste
3 C chopped cooked chicken
    breast

1 diced apple
1 small orange, sliced
1/3 C sliced green onions
2/3 C sliced celery
1 T chopped walnuts

Toss all ingredients together until well mixed. Chill for one hour and toss again. Serves 4.

66 LAKE TAHOE CHICKEN SALAD

A main dish salad for eight

6 cups cooked chicken breast, cut in cubes
2 ripe avocados, diced
3/4 C green pepper, diced
6 green onions with tops, sliced
2 C mayonnaise
1 C sour cream
4 T lemon juice
1/2 t cayenne pepper
salt and pepper to taste

Combine chicken, avocado, pepper and onions. Mix remaining
ingredients and pour over chicken mixture. Mix lightly with a fork
until blended. Sprinkle finished salad with paprika. Serve 8.

67 SHANGHAI SALAD

A low calorie delicious business

1 lb cooked, shelled, deveined
  small shrimp
1/2 head bok choy or iceberg
  lettuce, finely shredded
1/2 lb bean sprouts
1 C shredded carrot
3 stalks celery, sliced thin

3 green onions, shredded
1 T finely slivered fresh
  ginger root
1/2 C vegetable oil
1/4 C lemon juice
2 T soy sauce
2 t honey

Combine shrimp, bok choy, bean sprouts, carrot, celery, onions
and ginger in large bowl. Blend oil, lemon juice, soy sauce and
honey in small bowl; pour over shrimp mixture. Toss to coat.
Spoon shrimp mixture onto individual salad plates; garnish with
onion tassels. Serves 4.

68 SHRIMP SALAD

Your guests will love this

2, 5-oz cans shrimp, cleaned
1 C celery, sliced
2 hard-boiled eggs, chopped
3 T dill pickle, diced
1/2 C mayonnaise
1 T each: lemon juice and catsup
1 t Worcestershire sauce
1/2 C sliced black olives
salt and pepper to taste

Toss all ingredients together lightly. Serve on lettuce leaves, garnished with black olives. Serves 4.

69   SHRIMP AND PEAPOD SALAD

Make tonight for tomorrow's dinner

1 pkg frozen peapods
1/2 lb cooked shrimp
6-8 fresh mushrooms
4 green onions
1 pkg Italian salad dressing mix
white wine

Pour boiling water over frozen pods, drain and cool. Slice
shrimp lengthwise; slice mushrooms and onions. Mix salad
dressing according to directions substituting wine for water.
Pour all of dressing over all ingredients. Cover and refrigerate
overnight. At serving time, drain off excess dressing and add
freshly ground pepper to taste. Serve on lettuce leaves. Serves 4.

70 CHINESE CRAB SALAD

A main dish salad for eight

12 oz frozen or fresh crab meat
1, 10 oz pkg frozen peas
1 C chopped celery
1 small onion, minced
3/4 C mayonnaise
1 T lemon juice

1/4 t curry powder
1 t soy sauce
1/4 t garlic salt
1, 3 oz can chow mein
   noodles
1/2 C slivered almonds

Drain crab meat and break into large pieces; mix with peas, celery, and onion. Cover and chill. Combine remaining ingredients for dressing except chow mein noodles and almonds. Chill. At serving time, toss all ingredients together lightly.

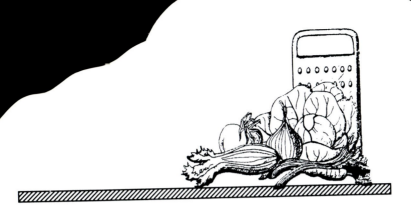

71 CAESAR SALAD

One version of a very old favorite

1 clove garlic
1/2 C salad oil
2-3 slices white bread
Parmesan cheese
1/2 head lettuce
1/2 bunch curly endive
1, 2 oz can anchovies (optional)

1 beaten egg
1/2 t salt
1/2 t pepper
1 t Worcestershire sauce
1/2 C Parmesan cheese

Put garlic through a garlic press and add to salad oil; let stand. Cut bread in cubes, spread on a baking sheet, pour a little of the garlic oil over them and bake at 225° until toasted and crisp. Sprinkle with Parmesan cheese. Break lettuce and endive into salad bowl and add croutons and anchovies. Strain salad oil to remove garlic and pour over vegetables. Combine remaining ingredients for dressing and beat well. Pour dressing over salad and toss lightly. Serves 6.

72   TUNA PEPPER SHELLS

2, 6 1/2 oz cans tuna, drained
2 C chopped celery
1 T each: Chopped green pepper, onion and pimento
3/4 C toasted pecans
1 C mayonnaise
2 T milk
1 T lemon juice
1 t sugar
salt and pepper to taste
2 hard boiled eggs, chopped
3 medium green peppers

Mix mayonnaise with milk, lemon juice, sugar, salt and pepper.
Toss dressing with other ingredients except whole peppers. Cut
peppers in half lengthwise, and remove seeds. Pile salad in pepper
shells. Garnish with egg slices. Serves 6.

73 CARROT POTATO STICK SALAD

Pretty, delicious, and good leftover

3 C shredded carrot
1 small onion, minced
1 C frozen baby peas
1, 6 1/2 oz can white tuna
1 C salad dressing
1 t vinegar
2 t sugar
1 t salt
1 small can french fried potato sticks

Mix carrot, onion, peas and tuna. Stir in salad dressing until mixture is moistened, but not too moist. Season with vinegar, sugar and salt. Just before serving, add potato sticks and toss lightly. Serve on lettuce leaves. Serves 8-10.

74 DIETER'S DELIGHT TUNA SALAD

Fill up on this tasty business with few calories

1, # 2 can diced beets, drained
2 C sliced, raw cauliflower
1/3 C diced onion
1 C sliced celery
1, 6 1/2 oz can water packed tuna
salt, pepper and herbs of choice
fat free salad dressing of choice

Combine ingredients and chill to blend flavors. Serves 2.

Pasta
Salads

75 CONFETTI SPAGHETTI SALAD

Try this basic recipe; add your own special touches

1, 8 oz pkg spaghetti or rotini, cooked
1 medium cucumber*
1 medium tomato
1 small onion
3 oz sliced pepperoni (optional)
1 pkg dry Italian salad dressing mix
1, 8 oz bottle zesty Italian salad dressing**
1/3 C grated Parmesan cheese

Break spaghetti in thirds and cook until done, but do not over cook. Peel and cut cucumber and tomato into small chunks. Dice onion. Combine vegetables with spaghetti; sprinkle with dry dressing mix and blend. Stir in bottled dressing, cover and refrigerate to blend flavors. Stir in Parmesan just before serving. Serves 8.

Vegetable variations: Cherry tomatoes, radishes, corn, zucchini, green pepper, broccoli, cauliflower, carrot slices or curls, frozen or canned artichokes, peas, olives and mushrooms.
**Try Catalina or French or dressing of choice for flavor variety.*

76 MACARONI AND CHEESE SALAD

1, 8 oz pkg macaroni of choice
4 oz medium or sharp cheddar cheese, cubed
1 C frozen green peas, slightly cooked
1/2 C sliced celery
1 small onion, finely chopped
3 T sweet pickle relish
1 t sugar
salt and pepper to taste
2 T chopped pimento
1 C mayonnaise

Cook macaroni and drain. Combine all ingredients and toss lightly. Adjust seasonings to taste. Serves 8.

77 MARINATED MACARONI SALAD

The pasta is flavored before mixing with dressing

3 C cooked macaroni
1 T vinegar
1 T lemon juice
3 T oil
1 t each salt, pepper
   seasoned salt and MSG
1/2 t garlic powder
1 T dried parsley (or fresh)

3 sliced green onions
1 C sliced celery
1 large green pepper, diced
1/2 C sliced black olives
6 hard boiled eggs, chopped
1 T sweet pickle relish
2 C mayonnaise (about)

Combine macaroni with vinegar, lemon juice, oil and seasonings; cover and refrigerate over night. Add remaining ingredients to macaroni, adding mayonnaise until desired consistency is reached. 8-10 servings.

78 FRUITY CHICKEN MACARONI

A good combination of fruit, vegetables and pasta

1 C cubed, cooked chicken
1/2 C uncooked macaroni
3/4 C frozen green peas
2 T diced celery
1 T lemon juice
1 C dark sweet
   cherries, or pineapple chunks

Dressing:
1/4 C sour cream
1 T mayonnaise
1 1/2 t lemon juice
1/4 t pepper
2 t sugar

Cook macaroni in salted water just until done; drain and rinse.
Combine macaroni, chicken, peas, celery, lemon juice and cherries
or pineapple. Mix dressing ingredients and fold into salad. Chill
for one hour. Serves 4.

79 CHICKEN & PEAPOD PASTA SALAD

Ginger for flavor, almonds for crunch

1 C salad dressing*
2 T soy sauce
1 t ground ginger
1/4 t hot pepper sauce (optional)
3 C (8 oz) rotini, cooked, drained

2 C chopped cooked chicken
1 C pea pods
1 C chopped red pepper
1/4 C sliced green onions
1/4 C slivered almonds

Cook pea pods until tender-crisp. Combine with chicken, pepper and onions. Mix salad dressing, soy sauce and seasonings. Add remaining ingredients and mix lightly. Refrigerate. Serves 8.

Use 1/2 cup unflavored yogurt and 1/2 cup salad dressing if desired.

80 CASHEW AVOCADO SPECIAL

A touch of lemon add zest to this delicious business

1 C cooked pasta of choice
1 1/2 C diced cooked chicken (also try with seafood)
1 C sliced celery
1 T lemon juice
1/2 t grated lemon rind
2 sliced green onions
1/2 t each salt and paprika
1/4 C white table wine
1 medium ripe avocado
1/2 C chopped cashews
1/2 C mayonnaise

Combine pasta, chicken, celery, lemon juice, rind, onions, seasonings and wine. Refrigerate and let stand for several hours to blend flavors. At serving time, cut avocado in half, remove pit and skin. Cut avocado in small chunks and toss with chicken and pasta mixture. Add nuts to salad. Mix mayonnaise into salad with fork,

adding more if necessary for desired consistency. Serve in crisp lettuce cups and garnish each serving with half a cashew.
6 servings.

81 GREEK PASTA SALAD

A savory blend of flavors to serve warm or cold

1, 1 lb pkg rotini noodles
1 lb boneless chicken, cooked
3/4 C sliced celery
1 sweet red pepper, chopped

2 C sliced ripe olives
1, 4 oz pkg Feta cheese
3 green onions, sliced
1, 16 oz bottle Italian
    dressing

Cook noodles and drain. Cut chicken in bite sized pieces. Combine salad ingredients with dressing. 16 servings.

82   CHICKEN PASTA STIR FRY SALAD

To serve hot or cold!

8 oz spaghetti, cooked
3 T olive oil
1 raw chicken breast
1/2 medium onion
1 small zucchini
1/2 red bell pepper

1-1/2 Italian seasoning
2 t parsley flakes
1 t salt
1/2 t garlic powder
1/8 t pepper

Cut chicken in strips, onion in narrow wedges, zucchini, and pepper in narrow sticks. In large skillet or wok, heat oil; add chicken and stir fry until no longer pink. Add vegetables and fry just until tender crisp. Stir in parsley, Italian seasoning, salt, garlic powder and pepper. Add spaghetti, toss to mix and heat until spaghetti is hot. Serve immediately or cover and chill. Serves 4-6.

83   PASTA TACO SALAD

Serve warm or cold

3 C elbow macaroni, cooked
1 lb lean ground beef
1 C chunky picante salsa
1 C taco sauce

1/2 head lettuce, shredded
1 1/2 C shredded cheese
1 1/2 C crushed tortilla chips
dairy sour cream
6 black olives

Brown meat and drain on paper towels. Stir salsa, taco sauce and cheese into meat. Combine pasta and meat. Just before serving, add tortilla chips. Make beds of lettuce on individual salad plates and pile pasta mixture on lettuce. Garnish each serving with a dollop of sour cream, and top with an olive. Serve immediately. Serves 6.

84 GOURMET DINNER SALAD

Lots of garlic and basil in this prize winning salad

6-10 cloves garlic, peeled
1/2 C walnut meats
1 C fresh or 1/3 C dried basil
1/2 C olive oil
1/2 C melted butter
1/2 C Parmesan cheese
salt and pepper to taste

1 lb linguine or fettucine
1/2 lb bacon or ham
6 stalks fresh asparagus
1 1/2 C fresh broccoli
2/3 C frozen peas
3 small zucchini

Combine garlic and nuts in blender or food processor for 30 seconds. Add basil and process again. Add combined oil and butter slowly until mixture is like paste; add cheese, salt and pepper. Cook pasta and drain. Cut bacon or ham in cubes and cook. Drain on paper towels. Remove most of drippings from pan and stir-fry vegetables for about 3-4 minutes, until tender-crisp. Toss meat, vegetables, pasta and sauce in a large bowl. Serve on individual plates. Serves 6.

85 HAM AND MOZZARELLA SALAD

A different and delicious combination

Dressing:
1 egg
2/3 C salad oil
1/2 C Parmesan cheese
1/4 C white wine vinegar
1/2 t each salt and pepper
1/4 t ground cloves
1 clove garlic

8 ozs rotini macaroni
5 ozs fresh spinach, torn
8 ozs ham, cubed
8 ozs mozzarella cheese, cubed
1, 4 oz can green chilies, diced

Cook and drain macaroni. Make dressing: Place egg in blender and blend for 5 seconds. With blender running, pour oil very slowly into egg and blend until thick; add remaining ingredients and blend until smooth. Mix dressing with macaroni and add remaining ingredients. Chill at least 2 hours before serving. Serves 6-8.

86 ROBYN'S SUMMER SALAD

"Hurry Mom, send our pasta salad recipe for the book"

1, 8 oz pkg thin spaghetti
2 C sliced spinach
6 ozs salami, thinly sliced
2 large carrots, coarsely shredded
1 medium yellow pepper, cut in strips
1/2 C grated Parmesan cheese
1/4 C olive oil or salad oil
1/4 C red wine vinegar
1/ t salt
1/4 t pepper
1/2 t dried oregano

Cook spaghetti and drain. Combine prepared vegetables with spaghetti. Combine dressing ingredients, shake to blend and pour over salad. Serves 4-6.

*For added zest, add a little Italian dressing to salad

87 SEAFOOD PASTA SALAD

Many favorite ingredients

8 oz rotini (corkscrew) noodles, cooked and drained
1 1/2 C crab meat, or seafood of choice
1 C broccoli flowerets
1/2 C chopped green pepper
1/2 C chopped tomato
1/4 C green onion slices
1/4 C parmesan cheese
1/2 C mayonnaise or salad dressing
1/4 C Italian dressing

Steam broccoli until tender crisp and rinse in cold water; combine
with seafood, other vegetables and pasta. Mix salad dressings
and cheese, and mix lightly into salad ingredients. Adjust
seasonings to taste. Serves 4-6.

88 TUNA AND PASTA STUFFED TOMATOES

3 C cooked elbow macaroni
1 , 6 1/2 can water packed tuna
4 slices light cheese, cut in pieces
1/2 C chopped green pepper
2 T chopped pimiento
6 T low or no fat Italian dressing
2 T lemon juice
1-2 T prepared horseradish
1/2 t garlic salt
2 T chopped fresh parsley (or 1 T dried)
6 medium vine-ripened tomaotes

Cut out stems and some of center of tomatoes; cut in wedges
nearly to bottom and open each tomato on a salad plate. Combine
remaining ingredients and pile on tomatoes. Serves 6.

89 VICE VERSA SALAD

Omit macaroni and tomatoes from salad above. Cook 12 giant
macaroni shells. Stuff shells with salad and garnish with tomato
wedges. Serves 6.

Relishes

90   PERFECT BEAN SALAD

A favorite to have on hand. Keeps well

1, 1 lb can green beans
1, 1 lb can yellow wax beans
1, 1 lb can kidney beans
1, 1 lb can small lima beans
1 green pepper, cut in thin rings
1 medium onion, cut in thin rings
1/2 C sugar

1/2 t dry mustard
1/2 t basil
1/2 C red wine vinegar
1 t salt
1/2 t dried tarragon
2 T minced parsley
1/2 C oil

Drain all beans and combine with onion and pepper rings.
Combine remaining ingredients and pour marinade over
vegetables; mix well, cover and refrigerate overnight. To serve,
lift vegetables from marinade with slotted spoon. Serves 12.

91 MARINATED VEGETABLE SALAD

Colorful and tasty go-with for sandwiches

1, 10 oz pkg frozen broccoli pieces, cooked and cooled

1, 8 oz can mushrooms, sliced and drained

1, 6 oz can water chestnuts, sliced and drained

1, 8 oz can sliced ripe olives

4 stalks celery

1 large green pepper

1 bunch green onions

2 C cherry tomatoes

1, 8 oz bottle Italian dressing

Cut celery in 1/2 inch diagonal pieces, slice green pepper and onion, separating rings. Halve tomatoes. Mix all vegetables in a large bowl, toss with dressing, cover and marinate several hours or overnight before serving. Toss again. Serves 6-8.

92   TABBOULEH OR TABOULE

A favorite salad from the middle east

1 1/4 C raw bulgar wheat*
4 C boiling water
3/4 C minced fresh parsley
3/4 C minced fresh mint leaves (some people use more)
3/4 C minced scallions
3 large tomatoes, seeded and chopped
3/4 C fresh lemon juice
1/4 C salad oil or olive oil
salt and pepper to taste

Pour boiling water over bulgar, turn off heat and let stand for 2 hours to soften. Drain very well so that water does not dilute flavor. Add remaining ingredients and let stand for several hours before serving.

Bulgar comes in different sizes. #1, or small bulgar is sometimes not soaked in water before adding to salad, but salad must stand longer for bulgar to soften. #2 bulgar must be soaked.

93 MARINATED ASPARAGUS

You'll love these delicious spears

1 lb fresh asparagus
6 T olive oil
4 T lemon juice
3 T white wine
2 T pickle relish

1 T chopped green onion
1 T capers
1 T chopped parsley
1/2 t each salt and pepper
1 clove garlic, minced

Cook, drain and cool asparagus. Pour marinade over asparagus in a glass bowl. Chill for several hours to blend flavors. Use as a relish or vegetable.

94 FRESH STRING BEAN RELISH

fresh green beans
Italian dressing or dressing of choice

Blanch green beans until bright green, but still crisp, Drain and cover with dressing in a glass bowl. Refrigerate overnight. To serve, drain off dressing. Serve with meat or fish.

95 SWEET AND SOUR CARROTS

1 lb carrots
1 medium onion, sliced
1 1/2 C sliced celery
1 bell pepper, sliced
1 C tomato soup

1/2 C vinegar
1/2 C salad oil
1/2 C sugar
1 t Worcestershire sauce
1 t soy sauce
1/2 t salt

Scrape carrots and slice 1/4 inch thick. Steam carrots until just tender. Place onion, pepper and celery over carrots. Combine remaining ingredients and boil until sugar is dissolved. Pour hot mixture over vegetables. Marinate for 24 hours before serving.

96 SUMMER TOMATOES

So simple and so good

4 vine ripened tomatoes
salt and pepper

2 white onions
fresh basil

Slice tomatoes and onions. Alternate layers in a glass bowl, seasoning each layer with salt, pepper and basil. Cover with plastic wrap and refrigerate for four hours for flavors to blend. Serve with any meat or fish.

97 PICKLED BEETS

2, #2 cans beets, whole or sliced
1 1/2 C vinegar
1/2 C water or beet juice

2 C sugar
1 t salt

Drain beets, reserving juice; combine remaining ingredients and heat drained beets in the syrup until boiling. Simmer for five minutes. Cool and refrigerate. Serve with sandwiches or cottage cheese. These keep indefinitely.

98 SAUERKRAUT SALAD

2 C sauerkraut, drained
1 C shredded carrot
1/2 C chopped green pepper
1/4 C chopped red pepper

1/2 C chopped onion
1 C sugar
1/2 C vinegar

Drain sauerkraut and rinse with water if milder flavor is desired; add other vegetables. Bring sugar and vinegar to a boil and let cool. Pour cooled syrup over vegetables and let stand overnight. Keeps indefinitely. Makes 1 quart.

99 PETER PIPER'S PICKLED PEPPERS

Some like them hot! Add Jalapenos to taste

12 whole green peppers
4 qts water
1/4 C salt
2 medium heads cabbage
1/4 C salt
1, 4 oz jar pimientos, diced
5 1/4 C sugar

6 C water
6 C cider vinegar
1 1/2 t whole cloves
5 sticks cinnamon
1 1/2 T whole allspice
1 1/2 t salt

Slice tops off peppers, save tops and remove seeds. Soak peppers and tops overnight in solution of 4 quarts water and 1/4 cup salt. Drain. Shred cabbage finely and sprinkle with 1/4 cup salt; let stand overnight then drain well. Mix pimientos with cabbage and stuff peppers. Tie tops on peppers with thread. Place stuffed peppers in an 8 quart crock. Combine sugar, water, vinegar and spices in sauce pan; bring to a boil and cook for 10 minutes. Pour hot solution over peppers and weight down with a plate. Marinate for at least one week. To serve, cut peppers in quarters.

100   FREEZER COLD SLAW

Always on hand to serve with sandwiches or fish

1 medium head cabbage
1 carrot, grated
1 medium onion, finely chopped
1 green pepper, finely chopped
Dressing:
3/4 C sugar

3/4 C vinegar
1/2 C oil
1/4 C water
1 t celery seed
1 t dry mustard

Shred cabbage very finely; mix with other vegetables. Bring dressing ingredients to a full boil and pour over vegetables. (Use a non-metallic container.) Store in refrigerator in glass jars or freeze. Keeps indefinitely.

101   CUCUMBERS IN SOUR CREAM

1 large cucumber
1/2 C sour cream
salt and pepper

1 medium onion
1 T lemon juice
2 t sugar

Combine thinly sliced cucumbers and onions with sour cream; season to taste with salt, pepper, sugar and lemon juice to taste.

102 CUCUMBERS IN VINEGAR

1 large cucumber
cider vinegar

1 medium onion
salt and pepper

Slice cucumber and onion thinly. Cover with water and 1 t salt.
Let stand for a few minutes. Drain salt water and add equal
amounts of vinegar and water. Season with freshly ground pepper.

103 ROCK RELISH

1 C cubed smoked sausage
1 C cubed cheddar cheese
1 C raw broccoli flowerets
1 C raw cauliflower flowerets
1 small red onion, cut in chunks
1/2 C whole ripe olives
1/2 C whole fresh or
    canned mushrooms

Marinade:
1 t dry mustard
1 t garlic powder
fresh ground black pepper
3/4 C red wine vinegar
2 T sugar
3/4 t herb seasoning
1/2 C oil

Marinate salad over night in a glass bowl. Serve with crackers.

104 CORN RELISH

1, 16 oz can whole kernel corn
1/4 C pickle relish
2 T chopped pimiento

1 T brown sugar
1 T vinegar
2 t prepared mustard
1/2 t salt

Drain liquid from corn into saucepan and boil until it is reduced by half. Add all other ingredients and simmer for 5 minutes. Serve hot with meat or chilled with sandwiches.

105 CRANBERRY RELISH

Is there Thanksgiving Dinner without it?

1 pkg cranberries
2 unpeeled oranges

2 unpeeled apples
2 C sugar

Remove apple cores, and orange seeds. Grind all fruits finely and add sugar. Chill.

106 PEACH PICKLES

Clove-studded beauties for a special garnish

2 qts small, fresh peaches   1 C cider vinegar
2 1/2 C brown sugar   whole cloves, stick cinnamon

Scald and peel peaches, leaving them whole. Push a clove into each one. Bring sugar, vinegar and cinnamon to a boil; add peaches and cook until tender, for about 10 minutes. Pack peaches into four hot pint jars, and fill with syrup. Put a piece of cinnamon in each jar. Seal jars, or refrigerate.

107 PINEAPPLE RELISH

2 1/2 C pineapple chunks, in syrup   1/2 t salt
2/3 C vinegar   8 whole cloves
2/3 C pineapple syrup   1 stick cinnamon
1 C sugar

Make a syrup of all ingredients except pineapple, and simmer for 10 minutes. Add pineapple, bring to a boil. Cool and refrigerate.

108 GUACAMOLE SPREAD OR SALAD

Serving Tex-Mex?

2 soft avocados
1/2 C mayonnaise
2 T minced onion
1 medium tomato, chopped

1/8 t cayenne pepper
2 T lemon juice
3 slices bacon, fried crisp

Peel and mash avacados; mix with mayonnaise, onion, tomato lemon juice and cayenne. Chill. Just before serving, stir crumbled bacon into mixture. Serve as a cracker spread, or serve over a bed of shredded lettuce as a salad. About 3 cups.

109 HORSERADISH SAUCE

1/2 C mayonnaise
1/3 C plain yogurt

2 T horseradish
1 T prepared mustard

Blend and chill. Serve with potatoes, cold roast beef and ham. Makes 1 cup.

Salad
Dressings

110 PINEAPPLE HORSERADISH DRESSING

6 T sweetened pineapple juice
2 T vegetable oil
2 T vinegar

1 1/2 t Dijon mustard
3/4 t horseradish
salt and pepper to taste

Measure all ingredients into small jar with tight-fitting lid; shake until well blended. Refrigerate until ready to use. Makes 1/2 cup.

111 RASPBERRY DRESSING

Invented for a no salt diet. Delicious!

1/2 C bottled raspberry syrup
1/2 C oil
1/4 C cider vinegar

Shake together. Do not cook.

112   FRUIT SALAD DRESSING #1

2 eggs
3/4 C sugar
1/2 C orange juice

3 T lemon juice
1 C sour cream

Mix first four ingredients and cook until thickened. Cool. Stir in sour cream. Serve with any fruit salad.

113   FRUIT SALAD DRESSING #2

1/2 C honey
4 egg yolks, beaten
juice of one lemon
1/3 C olive oil

1/2 t salt
1/4 t paprika
1 C whipping cream

Heat honey until hot and runny; remove from heat and rapidly beat in egg yolks, all at once. Return to heat and cook for about three minutes, stirring constantly with a wire whisk until mixture is thickened. Cool slightly and beat in lemon juice, olive oil, salt and paprika. Whip cream until stiff, and fold honey mixture into cream until blended. Refrigerate. Use as a dressing or fruit dip.

114 HONEY POPPYSEED DRESSING

Good on both fruit and meat salads

1/3 C honey
2 T lemon juice
1 T frozen orange juice concentrate
1 T dark mustard

3/4 C salad oil
1 T poppyseed
1/4 t paprika

Combine all ingredients in a jar and shake well.

115 LIME & MINT FRUIT DRESSING

1, 3 oz pkg cream cheese
2 T honey
1/2 C mayonnaise
1/2 C heavy cream

1/4 t salt
3 T lime juice
1 T grated lime rind
2 T chopped fresh mint

Combine softened cream cheese and honey. Whip cream and fold
into cheese; add remaining ingredients. Serve over pineapple or
any fruit mixture.

116 HERB & CHEESE DRESSING OR DIP

Perfect vegetable dip

1 lb low fat cottage cheese
1/4 C mayonnaise
1/4 C fresh lemon juice
1 T chopped tarragon

1/2 C chopped parsley
3 T minced onion
1 T Dijon mustard
1/3 C water

Process in blender or food processor. Makes 2 cups.

117 SEAFOOD SALAD DRESSING

Serve over any seafood salad combination.

1 1/3 C mayonnaise
1/3 C yogurt
1/2 C chili sauce
2 T horseradish

4 t lemon juice
1 t salt
1/4 t pepper
3/4 t Worcestershire sauce

Combine all ingredients. Makes 2 cups.

118 BLUE CHEESE DRESSING #1

1 C mayonnaise
1/2 C sour cream
3 oz blue cheese
1 t white vinegar

salt and pepper to taste
1 clove garlic, minced
2-4 T water

Crumble cheese into sour cream and mayonnaise. Add vinegar, seasonings and garlic. Thin to desired consistency with water.

119 BLUE CHEESE DRESSING #2

1, 8 oz pkg cream cheese
1 C mayonnaise
1 C buttermilk
3 oz blue cheese

1 t MSG
1 t black pepper
1 t garlic salt
1 t onion salt

Soften cream cheese; add mayonnaise, buttermilk and seasonings and beat until smooth. Crumble blue cheese into dressing.
3 cups dressing.

120 CREAMY CHEESY DRESSING

A nice hostess gift

2 eggs
2 cloves garlic
2 T chopped fresh parsley
1 C grated Parmesan cheese
1 C vegetable oil
2 T lemon juice
2 T water
1/4 T pepper

Blend eggs and garlic in blender; add basil, parsley and cheese and blend until smooth. With blender running, add oil slowly. Pour mixture in a bowl and stir in lemon juice, water and pepper. Thin with more water, if necessary after storing. Makes 2 cups.

121   COOKED SALAD DRESSING

Delicious dressing for cold slaw or potato salad

1 C sugar
1 T flour
1 T cornstarch
1 T dry mustard
5 eggs, well beaten
1 C milk
1 C vinegar
whipping cream*

Combine dry ingredients in top of double boiler; add eggs and milk and blend. Gradually add vinegar. Cook over hot water stirring constantly until thick. Chill.

Whipped cream to taste may be added to the cooled dressing for a good fruit salad dressing.

122   CATALINA DRESSING

A dressing with many uses

1/4 C sugar
1/2 C catsup
1/2 C vinegar
1/2 C vegetable oil
1/4 C finely chopped onion
dash cayenne pepper

1 t salt
1/2 t dry mustard
1/2 t garlic salt
1/2 t paprika
1/2 t oregano

Combine all ingredients in a jar, and shake until blended. Chill
and store in refrigerator. Serve over salad greens, green beans or
sliced tomatoes; also as a marinade or basting sauce for meat.
2 cups dressing.

123 BEST THOUSAND ISLANDS DRESSING

2 C salad dressing
3/4 C catsup
4 T sweet pickle relish

1/2 t Worcestershire sauce
2 hard boiled eggs
2 T grated onion

Chop eggs until very fine. Mix all ingredients. 3 1/2 C dressing.

124 COLLEGE DORM DRESSING

Remembered by many

1/2 C salad oil
1 C sugar
1/2 C vinegar
1/4 C catsup

1/2 C chili sauce
1 1/2 t salt
1 small onion, grated
1/4-1/2 t Tabasco sauce

Beat oil and sugar. Stir vinegar, catsup and chili sauce together
and add to oil and sugar; add salt and Tabasco (optional) and
onion. 5 C dressing.